Praise About the Author

"If there is one person I have known who could be mad and despondent at life and what it has thrown at her it could be Brandi. Within 24 hours going from a loving, caring, vibrant 17 year old young lady with national athletic credentials to fighting for her life. In this struggle I watched her relationship with Jesus not just grow but solidify. Brandi is more than an overcomer, she is a thriver! This is Brandi's life in times of trouble (loving, caring and vibrant, always thinking of others). I could not think of my life without her in it. Congratulations on your new book."

Pastor Bill Webster
Pastor, Entrepreneur, Realtor®, Appraiser

"Brandi is an amazing woman of faith. It was a joy to be her pastors for many years and then to see the amazing spiritual strength she had when faced with potential life-ending health issues. Her story is beyond inspiring and will build strong faith in all who read it."

Pastors John and Linda Stocker
Pastors

"Brandi Aspinall is an incredible talent! Grounded and solution-oriented, Brandi thinks on her feet. She shows up big as a leader of leaders."

Teri Wilber
CHt., CNLP
PLD Program Director

"Brandi and Mark are amazing leaders and humans. From the very first time I met them, I felt like we were friends forever. They bring value and energy to everyone they come in contact with.
I am very grateful for them and our relationship."

Scott Nordby
CEO, Berkshire Hathaway
HomeServices Innovative Real Estate

"So proud of you!! Brandi you are so human, experiencing the fear, the worry, the heartache. You face the questions about 'what if'" and 'what about my children, husband, and family?' Yet you never allow yourself to remain in that space. Your faith is immeasurable. You are such a strong example of what 'Overcomer' truly means. I admire you so deeply. If anyone can write a book about this, it is you. It is such an honor to be a part of your life."

Lora Nordby
CEO, Berkshire Hathaway
HomeServices Innovative Real Estate

"Brandi's passion for life and desire to encourage others has no limits. From hospital staff and nurses sitting and laughing in her room while enjoying Christmas cookies or her willingness to ask everyone stuck on the side of the road if they are ok, even if we are running late, she is constantly looking to share the HOPE that she carries. That's what this book is. It's her way of spreading hope, love, joy, and encouragement to the reader, no matter where they are or the situation they may be in."

Mark Aspinall
Realtor®, Superhero

"As a mom, it is amazing to watch God take over and make something good out of an intended "bad." Brandi is one of my true heroines in the Christian world. Her testimony of Christ inspires me everyday, and the supernatural joy and wisdom that God has given her is inspiring. She truly is fulfilling the Word God gave me during this time, 'she is living and NOT dying and testifying of Him in the courts of men.' She draws wounded and floundering people to the light in a way that amazes and astounds me. When the scripture tells us to love our neighbors as ourselves, it comes to life in her. I love you my 'Boots.'"

Pastor Linda Webster
Pastor, Entrepreneur, Prayer Warrior

"This was an amazingly powerful read! As someone who has worked in the human potential movement for the last 15 plus years and knowing Brandi personally, this is a true story of human spirit and faith that will allow you to identify those strengths deeply within yourself."

Todd L. Campbell
Owner, Todd Campbell Coaching

"Having been Brandi's pediatrician at the time of her diagnosis and watching her progress through much of her treatment, I was struck by her strong will, determination to come through her illness and, most importantly, her deep faith. She was then, and is now, an inspiration to me."

Dr. John Guenther
M.D.

"I watched the struggle from afar. I was attending university in Oklahoma and was going to come home to be a support to my sister, but she wanted me to stay in school so I honored her request. Anytime I was in contact or around Brandi during this time in her life, she was always encouraging others and walking with a positive attitude. She was an inspiration to all those who knew her."

Brooke Steven
Medicolegal Death Scene Investigator, Sister, and Friend

"I met Brandi Webster (Aspinall) in 1989 at the tender age of 8. She was full of spunk, energy, and the joy of the Lord. I knew then that she was one of a kind, and she is still the same today! What a privilege it was to be part of God's plan for the saving of her life and restoration. Brandi has never allowed anything to hold her back and has lived life to the fullest! Her compelling testimony will inspire you to invite Jesus into every area of your life, to know Him as Lord, and to live and leave a legacy."

Dr. Brenda Orndorff
M.Th., M. Div. D. Min.

"A serendipitous encounter is how I would describe my introduction to Brandi Aspinall. I will forever be grateful for the day that I met this miraculous human! I had the amazing fortune of meeting her at a real estate industry event. Her collaborative nature and optimism filled the room with an incredible and comforting energy! Little did I know that she had defeated the odds and would then take it to another level as life presented her with unbelievable obstacles. Truly an amazing spirit!"

Coey Howe
Sales Executive

"The first time I met Brandi, her smile, bright and positive spirit, and infectious laugh made me smile. I came to know her as a colleague and exceptional businesswoman, who cares fiercely for her family, clients and friends. Then I learned her story and was even more inspired by her positive outlook on life, conviction of her beliefs, and dedication to excellence in her work. I am lucky enough to know her as a friend, colleague, and business partner, and by reading her story, you will also feel that spark of Brandi light that will inspire you and move you forward."

Stacey Schalk
Realtor®, Entrepreneur

"When you read this book, you will be inspired to greatness walking with the Lord. I am 30+ years Brandi's senior, and she is my idol. I strive to live up to her example! Love this book!"

Carol Ellis

"I have had the pleasure of knowing Brandi for the past few years as we have a shared passion for helping families find their next home. Long before I read her book and had any idea about her amazing journey through life, not to mention her unwavering faith in God, it was clear to me that she was grounded like few others we meet in our everyday lives. Our shared experiences have not been without struggle or conflict but her ability to put others first and focus on what really matters has carried the day more than once. Her compass for doing right by others and her compassion is always front and center for others to see. She leads by example each and every day. I would ask everyone to read her story and look within to see what work you can do as you learn about family, faith and real-life superheroes."

Greg Fowler
Owner of Hero Inspections & Environmental

Emmy,
Can I just say — WOW! We have been on a journey together for a while — you are a blessing and a HOPE! I am so excited to see what your future holds!

GO

God Bless,
Brandy Aspinall

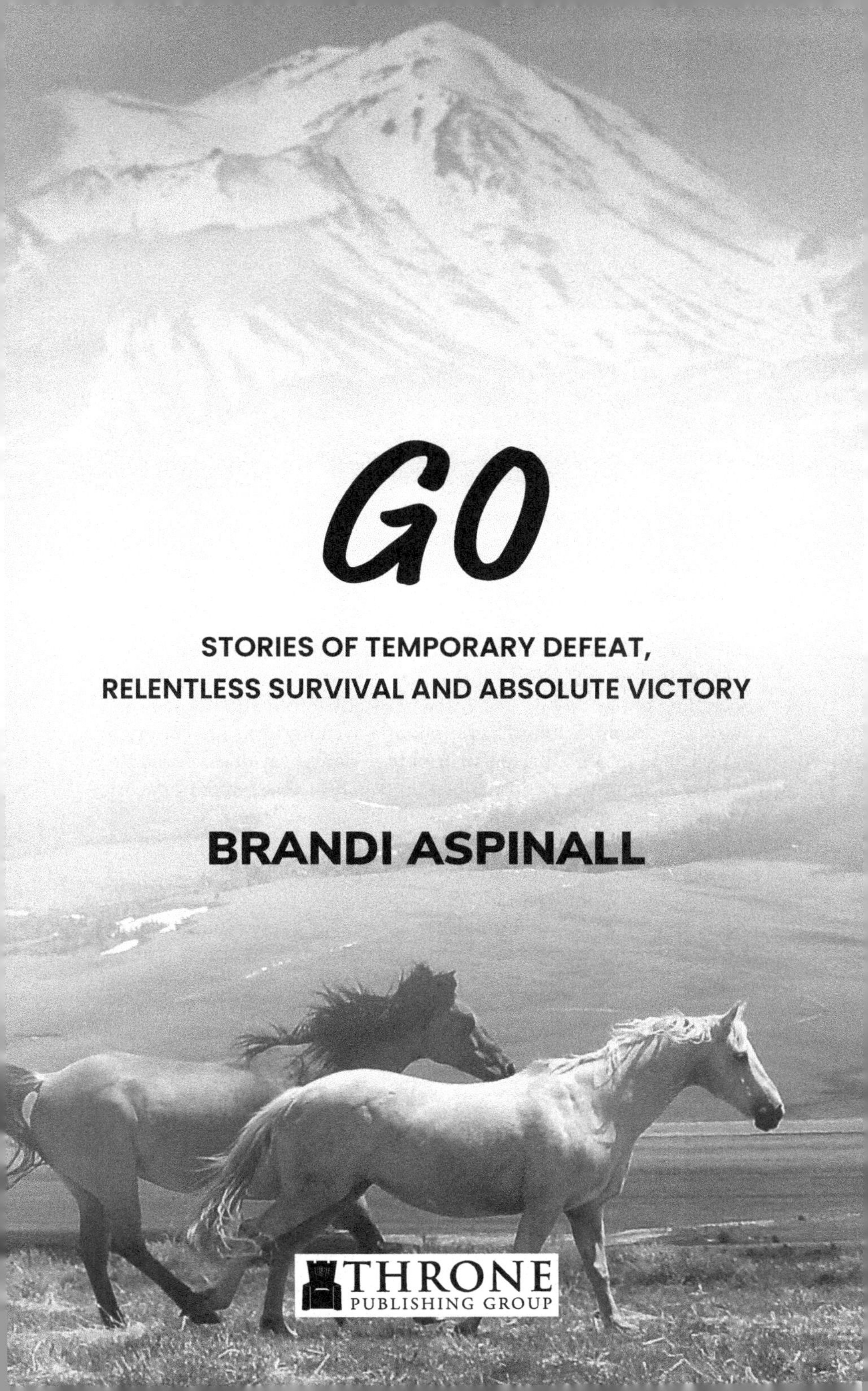

GO

STORIES OF TEMPORARY DEFEAT, RELENTLESS SURVIVAL AND ABSOLUTE VICTORY

BRANDI ASPINALL

Copyright © 2019 by Brandi Aspinall

Softcover ISBN: 978-1-949550-26-9
Ebook ISBN: 978-1-949550-27-6

All rights reserved. No part of this book may be reproduced or transmitted in any form or by any means, electronic or mechanical, including photocopying, recording or by any information storage and retrieval system, without permission in writing from the copyright owner. For information on distribution rights, royalties, derivative works, or licensing opportunities on behalf of this content or work, please contact the publisher at the address below.

Printed in the United States of America.

Although the author and publisher have made every effort to ensure that the information and advice in this book was correct and accurate at press time, the author and publisher do not assume and hereby disclaim any liability to any party for any loss, damage, or disruption caused from acting upon the information in this book or by errors or omissions, whether such errors or omissions result from negligence, accident, or any other cause.

Throne Publishing Group
2329 N Career Ave #215
Sioux Falls, SD 57107
ThronePG.com

Table of Contents

Acknowledgements . . . . *xiii*

Introduction . . . . *xv*

PART ONE: GROUNDWORK

Chapter 1 Rodeo Life 3

Chapter 2 Empty Stands 15

PART TWO: GET UP

Chapter 3 Moving Through and Moving Forward . . 23

Chapter 4 Find the Story 39

PART THREE: GO

Chapter 5 Your Inner Superhero. 55

Chapter 6 Honor Your Roots. 71

Chapter 7 What is a Home 83

Conclusion *97*

About the Author *101*

Acknowledgements

Throughout my life I have been surrounded by people who have loved me, supported me, and pushed me to be my best.

This book is dedicated to those people.

To my superhero Mark: I love and appreciate you more than you will ever know.

To my beautiful girls: I love and pray for you always. You inspire me to impact this world with the greatness of God's love.

To my dad, mom, and sister: I love and honor you for the foundation you instilled. It has inspired me to be the best version of myself.

To my prayer warriors in life: Thank you all for standing in the gap when all others saw the worst outcome possible. Your belief and faith are a big part of my journey.

To Jory: Thank you for pushing and encouraging me to take this step of faith.

To Shelly and Jeremy: Thank you for supporting me and making this book a reality.

GO

Finally, to my Lord and Savior Jesus Christ who has always proven to be with me every step of the way … to you I am forever grateful.

Introduction

The person we become is the sum total of our family history, our experience, our determination, and our relationship and reliance on God. My family and the legacy they've given me have taught me invaluable lessons, and I hope to teach my kiddos the same. Their faith, integrity, and the guidance they gave drive everything I do today.

Everyone has blessing and heartache, and no one is promised a life without difficulty. Early in my life, I learned to rely on and trust papa God for everything. There were struggles—sure. But whether winning rodeo championships or fighting for my life, I knew I was never alone. I am convinced there is always a reason to hope!

My life experiences could have caused me to give up, question God, or become bitter. I am not a therapist, and I don't claim to be an expert, but the lessons I learned on this journey of life may help you walk your own road.

Use this book and the chapter questions as you live your story, carry on your legacy, and establish your home. I pray you find joy, happiness, a sense of peace, and a deeper faith.

PART ONE

GROUNDWORK

CHAPTER 1

Rodeo Life

It seems I've always been in love with rodeo. Although, I'll admit, my love was more about the culture than perhaps my love of the sport.

My mom and dad were both pro rodeo athletes, so from a very young age, I was immersed in the culture. Early on I embraced the constant change that embodies the experience. Rodeo is a mix of long trips with large animals and continuous activity. It's early morning gas station food runs, late-night hotel room searches, brushing teeth in fairground bathrooms, and washing hair under fairground water spigots.

Whether your horse trailer has living quarters, you stay with friends, or in a hotel room, rodeo is about old and new family, character-building challenges, hard work, big adventures, fond memories, work, and laughter. It is a perfect mixture of all the things I love.

My parents always encouraged their children to do our best in every aspect of life—whether it was in sports, relationships, or life in general. Their message was that we are not here to win at the detriment of anyone else. They wanted us to strive to be the best we could be with integrity and commitment. So, that is what I did.

As a youngster I competed in, and won, many events, earning my first buckle at the age of five on my good ole barrel horse Hudson! At just seven years old, I tied my first nine-second goat run, won my first pole bending and ribbon-roping buckles at thirteen, and had my first two-second breakaway calf run at age sixteen.

There were certainly high points and accolades, but none of those came without work; I mean hard work every day! In fact, before I could get on a horse to rope a calf, I had to learn to rope a hay bale 100 times in a row. If I missed once, I had to start over.

Another way I improved was by working to be as strong and competitive as my sister. She was the best, so I paid attention to everything she did. I would practice what I'd seen her do and then challenge her. She usually still beat me and then point out how I could improve! Ha! Still, it made me want to improve. She was my inspiration.

As I got older, I began to focus on goat tying, breakaway roping, and barrel racing. By the age of thirteen, I was a world champion in goat tying. In high school, I won the Colorado State High School goat tying championships my freshman and junior years and multiple

Rodeo Life

Pro Rodeo barrel races on my barrel horse Humphrey. By my senior year, I had eight Colorado Junior Rodeo Championships between the junior and senior divisions and multiple All-Around Cowgirl titles. I was a four-time National High School Rodeo qualifier and set up with a full-ride rodeo scholarship to college.

Of the three events I competed in, my best event was goat tying. My goat tying horse Tuffy and I were an unstoppable team.

If you aren't familiar with that event, let me explain. Imagine sitting on your 1,200-pound horse holding a three-strand rope string in your mouth, staring down the arena at a goat that is tethered 100 or so feet away. You run your horse down the arena, dismount while the horse is at a dead run, and then catch, throw down, and tie any three of the goat's legs together. Oh … and to have qualifying run, the goat must stay tied for at least six seconds after you've backed away from it! The adrenaline was amazing!

Every event at the rodeo is planned out in a specific order, but there is *no* typical day at the rodeo. It's one of the things I loved so much about the experience! Generally, the day goes something like this. You get up at the crack of dawn to feed the horses, clean the pens, fill water buckets, and get your horse (or horses) ready.

Competition usually starts at about 8:00 a.m. with the national anthem and prayer. You check the order of

GO

events for the day to see when you compete and what animal you "drew" for the roping and goat tying events. Then, you would wait for your time to compete, all the while watching the ongoing events to gain some insight into the best way to compete.

Every moment revolves around preparation for the competition, and *everything* plays a role in the competition. Some things you control, but some you do not. For example, you have no control over the ground conditions in the arena, how the cattle shoot opens, or how far down the arena the goat is tethered. Yet any one of those can play a role in your time. Lack of control is "normal" for the rodeo.

Success was important, and it was good to win events I had worked hard at perfecting. But what brought me the most joy were the things that happened outside those wins.

When I was competing, I saw beauty in the gaps *between* the normal.

Bruised knees from hitting barrels, rope burns that needed tending, falling on my face in the mud after dismounting, or getting knocked out after being head-butted by a goat are all rolled into the same happy memory as trying to sprint away after a win to avoid being thrown into a water trough.

Rodeo Life

The simple joys of playing kick-the-can on the farm, family sing-alongs at the top of our lungs on long rodeo weekend trips, or sneaking out at night to lay on my horse and watch the stars are some of my fondest memories. All that hard work and competition? It was part of the world I love, so it was also part of the joy.

For me, the best experiences were the ones we had as a family—like waking up early to drive to the rodeos or sitting in the stands for my father's rodeo church service where my sister and I led worship. Our happy life consisted of baptisms in the same troughs where livestock had been drinking water over the weekend, the Bible studies my mom led at the trailer, or praying with other competitors.

Rodeo included singing the national anthem, riding in the "grand entry," watching storms rolling in on the plains, rounding up the cattle that got out on the highway, or watching the pickup-men and bullfighters challenge a bull that wouldn't exit the arena. But it also included celebrating each other's accomplishments, making friends from all over the country, working hard, laughing, and family being together.

The smell of a horse's neck, popcorn, and diesel are woven together with memories of competition and are what I remember fondly about the rodeo experience!

GO

My family has a natural competitive spirit, and I was raised to be a fierce competitor. It doesn't matter to us whether we are competing at sports or a game of spoons—we are serious! Playing spoons with my family did result in a few broken tables, and once, even a broken oven door! We are now banned from playing it at grandma's ever again! But win or lose, I was always encouraged to celebrate, improve, and to never win at someone else's cost.

Healthy competition is about moving forward and learning from your mistakes, embracing challenges with determination, and encouraging others to be the best they can be. My parents always encouraged me to compete against the best in my sport. They said to be the best, you have to compete against the best. We started slow, on older horses so we could work on our skills. When my parents were asked why they didn't mount us on "the best winning horses," their response was always that it is not about the horse, it is about skills. They truly believed it was about laying a firm foundation so we could win on anything we rode.

One of my fondest memories was at the end of the day when the air was cooling, the sun was setting, and a golden hue would stretch across the plains. My dad would say, "Girls, what time of day is it?" Our whole family would respond in unison, "It's my favorite time of day!" That was our reminder to relax, enjoy what we had accomplished, and anticipate the next sunrise.

RODEO CHARACTER

Looking back, I can see how the rodeo experience helped build my character. Through their example and expectations, my parents and sister played a big part in that by showing me the importance of responsibility, determination, and focus.

Since ultimately, rodeo *is* about competition, one way my parents helped me shift my focus when I messed up in an event was to push me to do "the 10%."

The 10% meant focusing on one small task for the day in a particular event. For example, in barrel racing, mastering the first barrel is key to winning. It's called the money barrel for a reason! If the approach is missed, the rest of the run is usually off.

Doing the 10% means rather than trying to improve the whole run, you concentrate on improving that one component. When you succeed in mastering the 10% of your approach to the first barrel, you consider it a win. Then, and only then, do you move to the next 10% for the rest of the run.

GO

The 10% is about improving small things and celebrating small wins. Focus on what you can do today, and it will lead to bigger wins. That approach to competition had a big impact on me back then, and it is still a concept I use today in my home and life.

Winning takes commitment to practice, and preparation for competition usually looked something like this. I would practice the 10% I needed to focus on, get the horse ready for the event, visualize the competition, take a deep breath, and focus. Then, when there were about five competitors ahead of me, I would take a deep breath and pray.

Competition can be tough, and it's easy to find reasons to be discouraged. Winning can end quickly if you hit a barrel, miss a calf, break out, or have a goat get up. My parents had me work on the 10% in each event. But win or lose, they always reminded me that my identity wasn't in the performance, but in Christ.

My junior year of high school, my average goat tying time for the year was 7.8 seconds. I was poised to win nationals and it seemed everything was in my favor, but it all ended during the first round at nationals. My goat got up before the six-second rule, resulting in a "no time" and bringing that championship dream to an end. Back at the trailer, I fell apart.

Rodeo Life

The frustration of that loss manifested in throwing saddles, kicking dirt, saying a few choice words, slamming trailer doors and crying … a lot. Picture a toddler's temper tantrum. But my mom's response was to go outside and pray. She came back and let me know it was time to bring it back in and remember what's important.

She prayed with me and asked me to decide if the loss was going to define me or if I could give it to God, learn from it, and move forward. I had my "pity party" and now it was time to work on my 10% and be grateful for what I had and had accomplished. I prayed and chose to move forward. That day, my mom instilled in me a true lifestyle of prayer and identity beyond the competition.

Later that day a young man came over to check on me, but it turned out he was going through a big loss in his personal life. I watched as my parents sat and read the Bible with him. He accepted Jesus into his heart and he was filled with joy! It completely changed his outlook and gave him hope.

It taught me something about life challenges. There will be times in life when your "goat gets up." You may not win, make number one in your company, or get to the top of the mountain. But you have to face the loss, give it to God, give yourself grace, move past it, and work on your next 10%.

GO

Praying became my way to glorify God behind the scenes and helped me put my focus back where it mattered—on loving God and loving people.

Here's an example of the way I prayed:

Papa God, surround this arena with your angels. Keep my horses safe. Keep me safe. And keep the other competitors safe. Let my life be an example to others of your love and let people see you in me.

Praying allowed me to work hard on my craft, improving 10% at a time, take the focus off myself and the performance. It helped me find ways to rely on God.

Questions to Go:

1. For me, it was the rodeo experience that helped build my character. What life experiences became the basis for what you do or believe?
2. What can you do, or give to God today that will lead to bigger wins? What is your 10%?
3. Praying helped me find ways to glorify God behind the scenes. Take a moment now to write down your own prayer. Ask Papa God to help you to glorify Him. Be specific.

CHAPTER 2

Empty Stands

EMPTY STANDS

During the rodeo, there is constant noise and commotion. There are clanging gates, tractors running, buzzers buzzing, and people yelling. The days are filled with constant "go" and always wondering, "what's next?"

If you compete in rodeo, you are always conscious of what you need to do and where you need to be. There is a constant awareness of what's going on, an intense focus, and a heightened sense of time and circumstances.

Then the competition ends, everyone clears out of the rodeo grounds, everything goes quiet, and it's eerily silent.

It was at one of those moments that Dad asked me to follow him into the middle of the arena. As we walked, it was a bit disturbing to feel how empty the rodeo grounds were. We stood in silence in the middle of the arena for a moment and then he asked me to look at the

GO

empty stands. I remember watching a piece of trash blow across the arena floor, hearing a horse whinny in the distance, and watching a small sparrow find its nest in the stands' rafters. Then a hollow, quiet feeling set in.

I had just won the state finals. I had dominated and was heading to nationals, again. I felt a huge sense of accomplishment and pride, so I was wondering, *why am I standing here?* We should be celebrating my great success! But we just stood in silence for a bit. I took in the scene, and I waited.

Then, he asked me where everyone had gone. I thought about it for a bit, and he pointed out that even though I just had a phenomenal state finals, it was done. Everyone I had competed against was on the road headed for the next championship or going home to practice and figure out how to beat me at the next rodeo.

He told me that after four or five years when I had moved past rodeos and the championship I'd just won, onto the next stage of life, everything I had accomplished in the flesh will be forgotten. Everyone will be thinking about who's on top at that time—not about me and my accomplishments.

My dad challenged me to think about the impact I make outside the rodeo arena and asked me what kind of legacy I had left with the people I came in contact with during that week. If they won't remember me for my accomplishments, what would they remember me for?

EMPTY SEATS—FULL LEGACY

Seeing the empty stands made me realize I had a choice. It made me think about my attitude, and the ways pride could creep in. I could see how easy it would be to live on moments of my success instead of moments that bring success to others. It's important where you put your focus and how you impact others.

That conversation with my dad didn't diminish what I accomplished at the state finals, but it *did* help me internalize a lifestyle of focusing on what really matters—those you help, lift, and encourage during the process. I learned it's important to enjoy your success, reflect on the process, and figure out what impact you've made for the better.

Every moment, whether you win or lose, you have a choice to stay stagnant, letting it define you, or let it inspire you to improve, to change, and to motivate others. It's about celebrating victories and letting your accomplishments, or failures, move you forward, living life to the fullest, and always asking God for His wisdom along the way.

GO

Success isn't found in wins or losses; it is in the lessons learned. It's about figuring out how we can impact this world with God's love. Whether you are at the top of your game, the bottom, or somewhere in between, I encourage you to do life with grace and kindness. Leave a legacy of God's love in people that impacts them for the better.

Rodeo taught me a lot, but my biggest lesson was this: Your identity is not in the championship; it is in God alone.

Questions to Go:

1. Success is temporary. God's love is eternal (Romans 8:38-39). What are two ways you can be an influence outside of what you do?
2. What difficulty or success have you allowed to define you? Ask God how He defines you.
3. How can you let your success or difficulty inspire you to improve, to change, or to motivate others? Ask Jesus to reveal how you already impact "behind the scenes."

PART TWO

GET UP

CHAPTER 3

Moving Through and Moving Forward

THE DIAGNOSIS

The devastating loss at nationals my Junior year could have defeated me, but instead of taking the loss as a failure, I chose to let it drive me to do better.

At the beginning of my senior year in high school, I was winning all three events—breakaway, goat tying, and barrel racing. About that same time, I started feeling weak. I had lost twenty-eight pounds in two weeks, had trouble holding food down, and my throat began to swell. Since my blood counts were fine, my doctor thought it might be an infection and recommended steroid treatments to reduce the swelling in my throat.

Within twenty-four hours, it seemed as though the treatment was working! Since the swelling had been reduced enough so I could eat, we decided to celebrate with root beer floats. I was very excited about having that familiar treat. That is, until later that night when I began to vomit. I continued to get sick through the night and into the next day. My mom decided I should go to the emergency room, but I made her wait until after the Broncos game. Boy was I stubborn!

By the time we got to the emergency room, I was in and out of consciousness, and my breathing was labored. I remember being covered in a warm blanket as the nurses took me to x-ray, but not much else, other than when Dr. Guenther walked back in with the results. I thought, *Wait, Dr. Guenther is here?* You see, he was my pediatrician and happened to be on call at the hospital. He had all the details needed because he had been at each step, in each examination, and now on call at the emergency room that night! What a blessing.

When he put my chest x-ray up, I remember seeing a big cloud of white across the image of my chest. I didn't understand the seriousness of that image, but I do remember seeing my mom put her head in her hands and sit down and my dad put his hand on her shoulder. I was so weak and tired, I just fell asleep.

The x-ray revealed a tumor the size of my hand filling my chest cavity. We found out the steroid treatment prescribed had reduced the swelling in my throat. However, it also attacked the tumor, causing it to kick out uric acid which crystallized and shut down my kidneys. I was immediately admitted to the hospital, where doctors started dialysis and scheduled a biopsy of the tumor.

On November 17, 1998, at the age of 17, I was diagnosed with Acute Lymphoblastic Lymphoma, specifically in the T-Cell (white blood cell). The tumor went around my heart, my ribs, and my lungs, which meant surgery wasn't an option and chemotherapy was in my future, if I survived the night.

The fight for my life began.

Although I knew the diagnosis, I didn't fully understand what it meant. All I wanted was to get back to singing, back to school, back to friends, and back on a horse. I wanted to join my sister on her rodeo team in college and my greatest wish was to run barrels at the National High School Finals Rodeo just once more. I had a phenomenal horse, Humphrey, and loved riding him more than any horse I had ever ridden.

In retrospect, I believe not fully understanding was part of God's protection, because all I felt was peace—no fear. It was the Philippians 4:7 "peace that surpasses all understanding" that can only come from His protection.

In God's beautiful plan, I was covered in prayer right from the start.

Within the first twenty-four hours, an international ministry pastor called my parents because he'd heard I was in the hospital. My father explained what

GO

was happening, and he said to let me know, at that very moment, prayers were being said for me. He promised that by the end of the day prayers would be said all around the world.

The same day, a group from Bikers for Christ, out of Ft. Collins, Colorado, also heard about a little girl who was just admitted to Poudre Valley Hospital and in serious condition. They headed for the hospital. Just picture that! A group of ten to fifteen hard-core bikers coming to the hospital, surrounding my bed, anointing me with oil, and praying!

For the first few days, I was on dialysis. I wasn't keeping anything down. There was no improvement, and the kidney specialist told the nurses to "watch this family" because he had never seen someone with my kidney diagnosis recover.

The next night, a close friend of the family walked past the nurses, past my parents and into my hospital room on a mission. With no knowledge of my condition or diagnosis she sat in a chair and began to pray. She prayed from 10:00 p.m. to 1:00 a.m. the next morning. When she finished praying, she told my parents, "It is finished!" and left with no explanation! The significance of that statement would manifest the next day.

The morning after, I asked for seltzer water mixed with cranberry juice and was able to hold it down. My

Moving Through and Moving Forward

kidneys started functioning, and my blood counts stabilized! Are you kidding me? Sounds like something out of a movie, right? But it's true, and I lived it!

Later, a classmate came to visit and told my parents her mom had dreamed. She saw me lying on a bed and proceeded to describe my hospital room in detail. In the dream, her mom saw a woman praying in the corner of the room, the stained-glass window, and flowers sitting on a table. But most incredible was the very large angel standing at the foot of the bed! After a time, she said the angel spread out his wings so they covered the entire room.

This woman's dream was the same night the family friend had prayed over me!

A few days passed and the friend who prayed came by to clarify the "it is finished" statement. While heading to the hospital on that critical evening she had driven the same road many times, however, this particular night a sign she had never seen before stood out to her. It was for a motorcycle shop. It had huge angel wings on it and in bold, blue, neon lights the word VICTORY. She knew then there was a battle to be won. While praying she saw in the sprit a large angel at the foot of my bed. When released from prayer stating "it is finished," I looked at my nurse and asked if I could go to the bathroom. Wow!

Ephesians 6:13 says, "Therefore take unto you the whole armor of God, that you may be able to withstand in the evil day, and having done all, to stand." (NKJV) The word "stand" means to "be" or "abide." When you have no other answers, rest in Him.

I wasn't able to do anything on my own. I was lying on that hospital bed, and everything seemed to say my life was headed for the worst possible outcome. But God intervened, gave me His armor, sent in warriors on my behalf to fight while all I did was "stand" and rest in Him.

Seriously! Can I get an AMEN?

For the next few weeks, I spent time enjoying visitors, decorating my hospital room, joking with the nurses, and visiting other patients. I even named my IV stand "Flerbert!"

I figured that if he was going to be at my side morning and night, lulling me to sleep with his deep buzzing, or waking me up with his loud beeping, he was going to have a name. "Flerbert" it was!

This fight was different than any battle I'd been in before. I wasn't fighting for a championship or a buckle—I was fighting for my life, and God began to show me His nature. He sent an army to pray for me. He fought on my behalf. While I was able to do nothing, He did everything.

One night I opened my Bible to Psalm 103. It's a Psalm of Praise for the Lord's mercies, and I held onto

Moving Through and Moving Forward

it! God used others to love me and my parents through a time of despair.

The next night, as my dad was leaving the hospital, he encountered a group of kids smoking and cursing. It made him angry, and he thought, "Why my daughter? Why does she have to fight for her life and not them?" He shared later that God answered, "I love them, too." It was a reminder that God loves us no matter what we are doing—or *not* doing!

The medical staff predicted I wouldn't make it past the first few days and if I did, I would be in the hospital 5–10 weeks. God's response to that was having me walk out of the hospital exactly two weeks to the day—on my dad's birthday!

Since my kidneys were functioning properly, chemo started. I completed two chemotherapy treatments, and a few weeks later, when the follow-up x-rays came back, the doctors were mystified. Not only was there no tumor, there wasn't even evidence I'd had one. After chemo, there should be a dead sack where the tumor had originated, but there was nothing. Plus, my kidneys were still functioning as any healthy 17-year-old kidneys should!

My cancer was gone. I'd gone from a deathbed to fully whole in weeks. It was a victory!

Still, the doctors encouraged me to continue with treatments, so I did. My parents continued to pray

GO

for wisdom for the doctors and protection over me. I continued to go to school, sing, and rodeo.

As it turned out, this was the first of three near-death encounters. It was the second that marked the beginning of a very personal challenge.

During treatment, my blood counts began to concern the doctors. I had pneumonia with a white blood cell count as low as an AIDS patient, which meant I had to be completely isolated. When friends, family, or my pastors came to visit, they were forced to stand outside and wear masks. Teachers sent assignments with my mom. She would read to me, quiz me, and then send the results back to school—all while wearing a mask.

I cried because I couldn't hug my parents, cried at the sight of my deeply bruised skin all the needle pricks had caused, cried at the sight of my deteriorating muscles, and cried at the way my lungs burned every time I took a breath. Mostly I cried because of the isolation.

Even though I was lonely, hurting, and mentally fatigued, that experience taught me something important. I began to understand that even when things seem bad, I am never really isolated. I sensed a hope and a calm that has stayed with me to this day. I learned that God *never* has to stand outside the room!

Again, my blood counts corrected, and the pneumonia was healed. When I walked out of the hospital, for the second time, the doctors had no explanation for how it happened. Victory again!

MY CONVERSATION WITH THE DEVIL

My remaining chemo was to be completed as an outpatient treatment, which was fine by me. I had just finished my senior year state rodeo finals, so not a big deal! But I went in for the treatment and ended up losing ten days of my life.

It was the third time I'd had an encounter with death since I'd been diagnosed with cancer.

While receiving the treatment, I began having memory and cognitive issues similar to stroke patients. The doctors thought it was likely due to a viral infection and immediately admitted me because my brain was swelling.

My eyes dilated to the point that they looked pitch black, and I began to drool uncontrollably. My dad put it this way—the lights were NOT on and NOBODY was home.

The doctors began administering a cocktail of different antibiotics, but nothing worked. When my condition got worse, they decided there was a possibility it was a fungal infection.

However, the fungal treatment they would use had no counter-drug should I have any serious side effects from it. It was so dangerous, they only administered it as a last resort in the most dire situations. That drug was their last option.

Once again, I was at a crossroads. And once again, my parents prayed.

As I lay in the hospital bed, barely conscious, drooling, and being spoon-fed, a sweet aroma permeated the room and was noticeable not only to my parents but hospital staff. No one could figure out where the smell was coming from, but we knew it was the Lord.

One night my dad came to stay so my mom could go home, change, and get some rest. On the drive home, she heard God say, "Today, Linda, is the day your daughter will make a choice." He asked her to turn me over to Him. She desperately wanted to go back to the hospital but God said, "she's mine," and my mom surrendered me to Him.

At home, she fell on her face and had a deep encounter with God. She then had the most peaceful sleep she has ever had. The next morning, she awoke refreshed, and when she went back to her chair to pray, He spoke to her again. "Your daughter will live and not die, and she will testify of my love in the courts of men." She immediately pulled out her Bible to verify this declaration in scripture and read Psalm 118:17, which says, "I shall not die, but live, and declare the works of the Lord." That scripture gave mom a foundation and confidence that I would survive.

That very same morning, I rolled over in bed, looked at my dad and said, "Good morning, Daddy."

The flow of visitors slowed, and I was left to struggle as the doctors helped me regain my memory. I was thin and weak. My body was ravaged by the chemo. My skin was red, and my hair falling out. I was at a very low point, but was alive!

Then one afternoon I heard it.

Alone in my room, I heard an evil laugh. It was a deep, sinister chuckle, and I knew it was evil. It felt like my thoughts went dark, and it felt like the devil was showing me everything that was being taken away. My body was weak so I wasn't able to compete in rodeo. My lungs were ravaged so singing anything was difficult. My hair was falling out, I was black and blue, and I felt a million miles away from the girl I used to be.

I had a terrible feeling of dread, and I remember crying out to God and asking Him to help me.

Just then, I let out a powerful response to the enemy's attack. I remember boldly telling him that he could take all of it—my looks, my strength, my success, my family, my singing, whatever. But I made it clear that the one thing he couldn't have is my soul. I told him in no uncertain terms—that belongs to God.

At that moment, it was clear that my ability to fight was coming from a place deep within. All the lessons I learned growing up began to surface. I began standing firm on the foundation of faith my parents had instilled in me. I recalled the lessons of God's goodness like Luke 1:78-79—"Through the tender mercy of God ... to give light to those who sit in darkness and the shadow of death, to guide our feet into the way of peace."

As soon as I told the devil I belong to God, the conversation was done. It's like Deuteronomy 30:19 where we are asked to choose life or death. For me, life was the *only* choice. Victory again!

AFTER THE STORM

My father says that truth without experience will always remain in the realm of doubt.

Experience changes our perception and how we relate to God and our world. It presents choices at every turn. When things don't go the way we want, are we going to get angry or give up? When things go our way are we going to celebrate how we got there and lift others with us?

Moving Through and Moving Forward

Two weeks later, I was at the National High School Finals Rodeo running barrels! My mom had to help me on my horse Humphrey, and he took care of me during each barrel run. I sang at the national church service and gave my testimony of God's goodness.

Shortly after, a young woman reached out to me and told me that she had been there preparing to compete, and saw me sitting off by myself praying. She said it impacted her and encouraged her faith. I ended up hitting a barrel and didn't place for nationals, but I was alive, and God had let me experience my desire of running barrels at nationals! I just enjoyed being there knowing my family—and God—were cheering me on.

During times like this, I encourage you to pray. *Choose* not to focus on the hard things when tough times come. Celebrate that you are alive and know that you will help someone else in the future.

Easier said than done, I know! But I pray you choose to turn to God and just BE in him! Anything you're facing will be okay because there is always hope.

Questions to Go:

1. We all face difficult times in our lives. How can you focus on God's presence when you are lonely or frightened?

GO

2. Experience changes our perception and how we relate to God and our world. What experiences have changed how you see God? Remember He doesn't change! He loves you no matter the circumstance so ask Him to reveal His true nature to you.
3. It's not easy to rest when we find ourselves in the middle of storms. What can you do to choose to lean into and trust God when difficult times come?

CHAPTER 4

Find the Story

FINDING COMPASSION

Everyone has a story created from their past and present. Our pasts create who we are in the present, and our present creates who we are in the future.

When someone around us acts or reacts—whether in a good way or not—it affects us. Our experience and perceptions affect how we view that reaction. It's complicated because as Kris Vallotton put it, "We tend to judge others based on their actions, but we want others to judge us on our intent."

Situations can be as simple as someone's reaction to a conversation stemming from something that happened that morning. Or maybe it's because of something from their past that drives their fight or flight instinct.

Besides, what is a good or bad action or reaction? I am not a therapist, but in my life I've found people's *perception*, and their action/reaction, usually comes from

GO

their past stories. Things that influence our lives drive how we react *and* how we view others' reactions toward us. There are usually two stories—the one we make up in our head, and the one the other person has.

This is why we need to have compassion for others! Compassion is a huge part of our walk with the Lord. I learned this firsthand.

Before my cancer, I had a group of girls at the high school rodeos. We were inseparable. We did everything together and supported each other. We even knew each other's Taco Bell orders without having to ask! We knew each other's crushes, insecurities, and regrets. We celebrated wins and comforted each other in the losses. We were always there for each other. Or at least I thought we were.

At the hospital, I was keenly aware of who came to visit and who was absent. Sure, early on, there was some support—one came to visit, one sent a card, and one called a few times. But during the fight for my life, those friendships faded.

Walking out of the hospital was a victory, and I can still recall what I felt as we pulled into the fairgrounds for my first rodeo competition. I remember being so excited to see those girls. But not one came over to say hello, and they avoided me the whole weekend.

Find the Story

I was still very weak, and when I made my goat tying run, I fell to one knee on my dismount. I heard laughter and crumbled when I saw it was them laughing. I was shattered! I didn't understand what I'd done to deserve laughter and being made fun of, ignored, and mocked.

From my perspective, I was fighting for my life physically and just wanted to be somewhere that brought me joy to still be alive. That moment brought me hurt and pain. As a 17-year-old I couldn't understand why it was happening, but I formed a story that all friendship was fake. I believed they only wanted to be my friend because before the sickness, I was a champion. I didn't realize it then, but my cancer journey marked the end of these friendships, and it created a wall of resistance toward future friendships.

I never found out the "why" behind their actions, but a few years after high school, I got an apology letter from one of them. I was still so hurt I told myself it didn't matter. I told myself I was strong enough not to put any more effort into it. I had no compassion, no grace, and the wall I had created grew.

It wasn't until a few years ago when a wise woman asked why I never reach out for help, do everything on my own, and won't let friends give to me. She pointed out that I love to give but didn't know how to receive it. Wow!

GO

She challenged me to think about how much more I could give if I knew how to accept from others. We prayed, and I asked God for revelation. The story of my friends flooded into my mind, and I fell apart. I cried so hard I went through an entire box of Kleenex! At that moment, I clearly heard God ask me to forgive them for the perception I had. He also told me to trust His healing love and to forgive myself for turning away all other friendships.

Right then the walls began to fall.

I asked God to heal my heart, tear down that wall, and give me compassion and His love towards them. I had to choose to let Him heal my past so I could be open to His future for me. I wish I could tell you there was a fairytale ending and we all came back together and reconnected. It hasn't happened yet, but I can tell you that if presented with the opportunity, my heart is now in a position to accept that because of His healing compassion in my life.

Compassion is about taking time to understand your story *and* others'. It's knowing their perception and the feelings behind the situation. It's understanding how and why you are reacting as well. You don't have to be friends with everyone, but knowing both sides of the story helps you love the people that you or society may have rejected.

Find the Story

It means caring about other people and being willing to remove personal perceptions and feelings from the mix.

We need to move our crap out of the way and listen to the other side of every story. Remember, we can't judge someone's heart or salvation, but we can judge the fruit their life is producing to decide if we want to have deep relationships with them. We can point them toward God as a resource, mend the offense, and let forgiveness in.

I know some circumstances are more complicated than these examples, but it's best to take yourself out of someone else's action, remove your bias, and listen to the Holy Spirit. Understand what's driving the behavior—yours, and theirs. It doesn't mean you have to agree with the action or condone it. But why react, gossip, complain or let that action affect your minute, day, or life?

There's value in listening to someone with compassion because it gives you a positive mindset toward them. If you have compassion in everyday life, there is always a way to find the optimistic side of any story and put that situation in God's context. Besides, not having compassion is draining and steals your strength!

This concept applies to every aspect of life. In business, friendships, family, marriage, you name it. By applying compassion to every situation, you become a servant leader moving people with God's heart toward them.

GO

COMPASSION AT HOME

Compassion is necessary at home too.

You may not believe this, but I can honestly say my husband and I have never raised our voices or shouted at each other. However, one time, early in our marriage, we were running late to a dinner date. I was frustrated and so was he. I couldn't find a washcloth because the linen closet was so disorganized. I became very agitated and said something to the effect of, "AHHHH why are there no washcloths!"—not so slyly directing that comment to him. He then retorted, "Well, if someone would organize it." To which I promptly cut him off with, "Well, if someone would help out sometimes!"

Then, we paused and looked at each other and started laughing. We realized we were both about to escalate to a fight over a washcloth! HA! A *washcloth*!

Early on in our marriage we committed to have compassion for each other and before anything became a fight, we would pause, take a step back from the situation, and look at the full picture.

Look, it's usually not the dishes in the sink or the unfolded laundry that cause fights. Most of the time it's something else that's built up to that moment. In our case, we'd both had stressful situations at work that had compounded into everything running behind that day.

Find the Story

Mark and I have a time trigger and hate being late. It wasn't the washcloth that caused our "temperatures" to rise. It was the stories from that day. We were taking the day's stress into our time together. I was focused on getting myself ready, and he was thinking about what was taking so long. When we paused and took a step back, we realized it was comical to fight over a washcloth.

When you get to those moments, take a deep breath, and reflect on what's behind the moment. Then you can have compassion, remove the tension, and bring joy back to the relationship. I learned over time that if I give those difficult moments throughout the day to papa God, it removes the tension a lot sooner!

That particular situation did not begin with God's peace. Still, we allowed each other a few moments to be upset and not escalate to a full-on screaming match. Besides, let's be honest, I would have screamed, and he would have just stood there or walked away in anger.

We each knew the other had stress that day, and that allowed us to have compassion. Getting to a place of compassion let us move forward without a fight and showed how to care for each other in an authentic way.

My advice in these situations is to step back, remove yourself from the equation, and give up perfection. Remember, it's not all about you. In a marriage relationship, it is give and give, not give and take.

GO

Know that God has compassion for you in moments of weakness, so you have full authority to love others in their moments of weakness. There is no greater celebration than when His authentic love impacts the story.

SEEKING WISE COUNSEL IN STORIES

When I am in a difficult situation or dealing with someone I don't get along with, I give them the Tsar's blessing. It's a family saying we have adopted and comes from the opening song in the musical *Fiddler on the Roof*. The story is about the Jewish people in Russia, outside forces encroaching on their traditions, and eventually the Tsar's edict evicting the Jews from their village. The community rabbi is asked if there is a blessing for the Tsar. He replies: "A blessing for the Tsar? Of course, May God bless and keep the Tsar (he pauses) far away from us!"

Everyone has that one person in their life who seems to bring out the worst in them.

If a situation is not working, remove yourself from confrontation. If a relationship is causing you to be negative, it's okay to step away. We are called to love, but we are not necessarily called to get into a deep relationship with everyone. It's okay to love them from a distance and pray for circumstances to change in their lives.

Find the Story

You have to think clearly. To change how we perceive a situation, ask God to help you have His perspective.

Philippians 4:8, "Finally, brethren, whatsoever things are true, whatsoever things are honest, whatsoever things are pure, whatsoever things are lovely, whatsoever things are of good report; if there be any virtue, and if there be any praise, think on these things."

I once heard a story of a dad and his little son on an elevator. As the elevator got crowded, the boy got pushed to the back to the corner and all he could see were people's butts. Feeling overwhelmed and trapped, he looked up and said, "Daddy pick me up." When the dad picked his son up, his perspective changed. The son saw above the crowd, anxiety left, and he felt peaceful.

This story showed me that sometimes you just need to look at the situation you are facing differently. If you ask for God's perspective, He will intervene to change the view and the perceived circumstances surrounding you. Whatever situation you are facing can be brought back into God's presence, grace, and peace. The situation may not change, but your perception can!

If you are struggling, get the perspective of someone you trust. Go to the person who has Godly authority in your life. If you don't have that person, you should!

GO

Everyone needs to have a teacher in their life! You need a person who can pick you up and show you God's perspective. Timothy had Paul to guide, protect, and cultivate him in his spiritual walk. You need to go to your "Paul" for guidance. This teacher must be someone you can trust as an authority in your life. That person should be wise in the knowledge of scripture and have a passion for the love of God. You don't want someone who sympathizes with you, gossips, or condones the situation. The person you need will always point you to Jesus.

And, I have to say this—remember, guys mentor guys and females mentor females! This is so important! You are trusting and going deep with this individual. Those situations can get intimate, so the relationship should be handled with appropriate awareness.

Finally, in every situation and relationship, before you react or form a feeling, don't forget to look in the mirror. You may be responding from something that comes from your back story and is familiar to you. Perhaps the situation (or the person) is bumping up against your trigger and all you're seeing is butts. Ask God for discernment. Wait for the answer from Him. Then, when revelation comes, remain in your quiet place until you have peace. That way you can approach the situation with *His* wisdom and *His* word.

Find the Story

Right now, take a moment to think about your story. What is the internal dialogue when you read these words? What are you telling yourself? Are your thoughts positive or are you fighting negative thoughts?

Read Philippians 4:8 and ask the Holy Spirit for revelation of why you are having that reaction. Write down what you are hearing, feeling, or sensing, and let God set you free from any negative mindset so you can move forward.

Your understanding of who God is will influence your reaction and opinion, so you must choose to base your reaction on the foundation that God's love and compassion overwhelms a multitude of sin. Once you do, you can take that foundation, impact others, and lead others into His healing.

Out of all of this, the most important advice I can give you is to talk with God and read His word. Repent and forgive others and yourself for what was done, said, or thought. God will work on your heart, taking you from glory to glory. "Repentance" actually means turning around and walking away from sin. "Sin" simply means missing the mark, and we all play our part in every situation!

Finally, every situation is unique. Every situation is different. God's word and wisdom are the ultimate guide

GO

to life healing and a deep understanding of others' stories and most importantly, your own.

Questions to Go:

1. Things that influence our lives drive how we react, and how we view others' reactions towards us. What are two or three experiences that have influenced you?
2. In every relationship there is potential to get hurt. Where have past hurts caused you to put up walls of resistance? Ask God to help you pull down the walls you have created.
3. There's value in listening to someone with compassion. What are some areas you could have a more positive mindset towards others? Ask God to help you find a more positive mindset.

PART THREE

GO

CHAPTER 5

Your Inner Superhero

MY SUPERHERO

After college, I had the best job ever! I ran around with superheroes and childhood cartoons. I rode extreme rides, sang the national anthem almost every morning, and had funnel cakes at my beck and call!

I was an event coordinator for Six Flags in Denver. At that same time my husband, Mark, was a youth pastor and took a summer job at Six Flags to supplement his income. He played the Green Lantern and entertained visitors to the park as a superhero!

Although we both agree on the fact that we worked for Six Flags, we have different versions of *how* we met. *I'm* sure we met at a birthday party we both attended. But *he* thinks we met at a friend's going away party a few months before.

Regardless, before Mark, I had gone through a difficult relationship. By the time we met, I was busy climbing

GO

the corporate ladder and didn't think I needed the distraction of a man in my life. The only time I even thought of him was in context when I asked, "Where the heck is Batman and The Justice League?" for an event at the park.

Let me start at the beginning of my recollection of our first meeting. At the time, I had gone out on a few dates with the guy that played Batman at the park. Yes, I was dating Batman! It wasn't serious though. At some point I was invited to a birthday party for the manager of entertainment at the park, so I went.

When I walked into the party, I saw Wonder Woman in the corner crying, Batman rushing out the back door, and Robin coming around the same corner to say hello to me. Apparently, Batman had brought Wonder Woman to the party as his date but was trying to date me at the same time! Imagine!

Anyway, when I figured out what was going on, I told Batman to take a long walk off a short pier and enjoy the ride. I liked Wonder Woman, she was a great person, and didn't deserve this treatment either. I told him, "I want you in my life, but I don't need you in my life" and promptly walked away without giving him a chance to say a word. Oh, how well I reacted to drama and conflict (I say sarcastically)!

I was trying to act cool and not look upset, so I went outside to cool off. The Flash, Green Lantern, Tweety, and

Your Inner Superhero

Sylvester were hanging out on the porch, so we all chatted a bit. In case you are wondering, they weren't in costume. Still, it's fun to use their characters rather than their names.

When Mark (also known as the Green Lantern) started talking about being a youth pastor and his heart for ministry, it caught my attention. I mentioned I was cold and he put his arms around me. It was at that moment I decided I needed to leave. I had just told one guy to take a hike and now I had butterflies over another? What the heck!

For the next few months, I stayed away from all entertainment staff, except in a professional manner. Like I said, the only time I thought of Mark was when I needed him and the Justice League for an event.

Then we got news that Six Flags was selling the park. With that sale, they were doing away with all the Warner Brothers and DC Comics entertainment for all my events. The scramble to appease clients was on. I got busy, and Mark's employment at the park was ended.

It was a year before Mark came back into my life.

A call came from Batman. He asked for forgiveness and over lunch, he told me that he and Wonder Woman wanted to reconnect. We'd all been friends before the drama, so I was okay with it. They asked if I wanted to go to a Bible study they attended with some past park employees. Turns out it was at Mark's house!

GO

The minute I saw him, the butterflies returned. Mark eventually asked me out and ironically, our first date was to see Spiderman 3. I fell head over heels for him and married me a superhero!

The thing is, I had tried relationships without God in them, and it only made me bitter. I wanted nothing to do with the drama and was shut off to emotional intimacy. By the time I reconnected with Mark, I had turned that area of my life completely over to God. He put blinders on me until the day I walked into Mark's home. God knew just what I needed to redeem the many mistakes I had made. He knew I needed a superhero to love me through my hurt, insecurity, and self-doubt. God gave me that in so many ways when he brought Mark back into my life!

Mark is an inspiration and my biggest supporter. He's strong, stable, compassionate, gets along with almost everyone, and cares deeply for people. Things that normally don't move men move him. He's a strong leader whose talent and wisdom come from his complete love of Jesus.

He gives me strength and love. When I am ranting—as we females do—he brings stability. When I make mistakes, do something wrong, or say something I shouldn't, he doesn't let it rattle him. On the other hand, when he's going through something, he doesn't mind if I ask him what's going on because, face it, we females have to "talk about it!"

Mark is the family leader, a phenomenal husband and father, and a safe place for us to fall. If I'm having a bad day, all he has to do is put his arms around me and it settles me.

We walk through life together, and he rescues me when I need it. He does all this because he is submitted to the ultimate superhero, Jesus.

Plus, he's sexy and attractive—just like a superhero should be!

YOUR OWN SUPERHERO

All I can say is it seems like our entire relationship revolves around superheroes, and people often ask why our family likes superheroes so much. Well, in part I think it's because we see so many of God's traits in the heroes. The impossible becomes possible in Him! And let's be honest, everyone needs a hero.

As Christians, Jesus is our hero, and I believe He also places other heroes in our lives to look up to. The characteristics you see in the beloved superheroes on screen, in books, and in comics reflect characteristics of who God is and who He is in us.

GO

I also believe *everyone* is a superhero to those around them. That is reflected in the abilities shown in onscreen superheroes. For example, the Green Lantern's ring grants the wearer incredible and incomprehensible powers and abilities by harnessing willpower. That is similar to the power we receive from the Holy Spirit to face situations that seem impossible. If you read or watch the movies from that perspective, you may be able to understand why we believe God created us to BE—through Him—superheroes!

God's love is a superpower that we can harness to change this world. We are living examples of His love. If we understand we are made in His image, then we know that we get our identity from Him. He made something unique and created us with joy, love, and power!

He created us to have power through the Holy Spirit, and to be servant leaders who make the impossible possible. We're designed to be on the front line in the battle. Just like superheroes. We head into storms when others won't because we know God is with us and we have the Holy Spirit's power to make the difference.

Experiences *make* us superheroes. Every superhero has an origin story that creates who he or she is. God uses the experiences in our origin story to makes us steadfast and content.

When we know who God is, it gives us strength to stay the course and hope, which is a future expectancy of good fortune. With God, there is always a reason to expect more. Just like it says in Philippians, we can do all things through Christ!

Every superhero's identity is challenged at some point. There is always a moment when they must resolve to complete the task at hand and a choice to be who they are called to be. It's the same for us. Our choice is knowing that within us there is God Power that makes us victorious.

This scripture from Philippians comes from Paul's writing to encourage the believers. He says he knows how to live in abundance or lack. He knows how to be full or hungry. He is writing this from prison in Rome, typically located in the sewer systems of the city. Here is Paul, in prison, standing in sewage, telling others he is content whether he has everything or nothing.

We need to *know* who we are in Christ despite our circumstances. When hard times happen—and they will—we have a choice. We can fail forward into His grace or stay in our failure. Understanding who we are in Him helps us rise to the challenge.

During my experience with cancer, I knew God's love for me. So, living or dying, I knew everything would be okay. That's the kind of confident hope we can hold onto.

God made us to be His superheroes for those around us who may be in desperate situations. We are all called to defend the defenseless, love the unlovable, and take care of the widow and the fatherless. Just like comic book heroes, all is conquered in the passionate, unfailing love given to others.

Through Christ, everyone can be a superhero and use their "powers" to help others. When we help others, we give something greater than ourselves.

John 15: 10-13, "If you keep My commandments, you will abide in My love, just as I have kept My Father's commandments and abide in His love, these things I have spoken to you, that My joy may be full. This is My commandment, that you love one another as I have loved you. Greater love has no man than this, that he may lay down his life for his friends." And isn't that what a superhero does?

SUPERHERO FORMULA

The "**POW**er" formula is this. Dunamis (Dynamis in the Greek) + The Word of God + Prayer + Your Gifting + Your Choice = Your Superpower.

There is something inside superheroes that drives them to win in times of weakness.

Dunamis is the Greek word for power and used in conjunction with the Holy Spirit throughout scripture.

It is God-given **POW**er. It's dynamite power—explosive, earth-shattering, mountain-moving, death-conquering power! It's power in spite of our weakness or others' weaknesses. And it all starts with understanding who God is in us.

Some people believe Dunamis power is gone today, but I don't believe that! There is a greatness inside of you waiting to be ignited. Today, just like in the early church, the Holy Spirit is here to help us find physical, emotional, and spiritual victory. I've prayed over people and seen them healed from major medical issues, relationships mended, and set free from addiction. It's God *using* me as His superhero.

When I had cancer, he used others to pray over me, and we saw many victories. Doctors can't explain why I am still alive today. The word of God states He has given us this power to walk in His hope, joy, and peace.

> *Romans 15:13, "Now may the God of hope (the future expectancy of good fortune) fill you with all joy and peace in believing, that you may abound in the hope by the power (Dunamis) of the Holy Spirit."*

Christianity is not to be lived passively—it's an amazing adventure to be embraced. **POW**er is released in our calling to be a superhero in Him. I always say,

GO

"God likes to show off." So, I pray He uses my legacy of His love to do so.

Understand, it's a choice. We have to choose to be used by and for Him. God never forces anyone into this choice.

The basic steps to receive Dunamis power for victory in your life:

- First, accept Jesus as your Lord and Savior. He was sent to save the world to conquer all sin and released the Holy Spirit into our lives. Allow His love into your heart. Circumstances may not change at that moment, but this choice brings a transformative experience that comes with an overwhelming peace and joy. It is priceless! When you ask Jesus into your heart, you receive the Holy Spirit as a gift.
- Second, Get into the word of God. Pray and let the Holy Spirit reveal God to you as the one to trust with the vision for your life. Know Him through His word, learn how He operates, understand that He is your best friend. Learn to ask for His help when faced with tough times. Trust in (choose) His ability, not your own. Then you will begin to see this **POW**er activated in your life.

Our POWer should always be used to bring people into the presence of God. His presence gives us life and life more abundantly!

Allowing the Holy Spirit POWer to add to your gifts, skills, and passions confounds logic, and miracles happen. If you want to know what your gift, skill, or passion is, ask yourself these questions:

What are you good at? What values do you hold onto? What are you passionate about? It's usually a natural interest that draws you in or a life circumstance that created a passion in you for it.

What do others see in you: Ask those close to you where they've witnessed the gifts in your life. Maybe someone has said "you are very good at ...," or why don't you do (fill in the blank) you seem to have a gift for it.

What do personality tests say? There are several assessments available to help you figure out your gifts. One example is 16personalities from NERIS Analytics Limited.

What did you love to do before you "had to make ends meet?" Did you want to dance, sing, make jewelry, teach, organize, build, create in any way, write, play music, fix things?

Gifts are strengthened when you work on your skills. There's a saying dating back to the 14th century

GO

that a jack of all trades is a master of none, but oftentimes better than a master of one. Work on your skills one at a time. Be a jack of all trades and work on the skills that add to your gift, then give them over to God for Him to infuse POWer and use you as a superhero to testify of His love.

Also know, we are not perfect, we all have weaknesses, and tough circumstances always show them. We can grow the most in these times. We're all human, but don't let the dark moments stop you! Instead, give weaknesses to God, and let Him work on it. Remember, He works *through* our weaknesses for His glory. I saw that in my life. I made more of an impact when I was fighting for my life than I did in all my rodeo championships! Let me be clear. He did not give me the sickness so I could learn a lesson. The cancer was a blatant attack on my life, but when I gave the fight to Him, He infused Dunamis and created beauty out of it that can only be described as a miracle.

One last thing. You can't just fight. You need to rest in God's presence. As a family, we would travel to and compete in about forty rodeos a year. My sister and I played volleyball and soccer, and sang at different events. We were a busy family and each activity required its own practice time. However, my family believed there is always time to rest.

Your Inner Superhero

You have to step away, rest, and thank the Giver of the gifts. It's easy to get so focused on your gifts that you forget to do that! But even Jesus removed himself from the crowds to pray and get rested. If you only have enough time to take a deep breath and say a quick prayer, do it. Get into the habit.

God is not cookie cutter. He provides for every aspect His children need—including rest. Figure out what it is that you need. Is it food, health, vision, water, or sleep? Create a habit of resting in Him and asking Him for strength.

In every situation, He will revive and restore you!

Ask yourself these questions:

- When do I rest the best?
- When am I the most rested?
- How can I rest more and make this a habit?

Finally, add the elements up. Dunamis (The Holy Spirit POWer) + The Word of God + Prayer + Your Gift + Your Choice = your superpower to impact this world!

Questions to Go:

1. Many times, we try to make relationships work without God. What are some ways God changes relationships?

GO

2. When we get our identity from God, we understand we are made in His image. What are some specific traits God gave you?
3. In what ways are you allowing the Holy Spirit to give **POW**er to your gifts, skills, and passions?

CHAPTER 6

Honor Your Roots

Your family legacy *is* important. Legacy is found in past generations. It's the history of your ancestors and what they have passed to you. It's handed down from generation to generation. It's the memories, connection to certain smells, sounds, songs, and sayings that attach to your emotions and build who you are. My family legacy is deeply rooted in who I am and directs decisions, influences interactions with others, and plays a part in my daily life choices.

THE WHISTLE

My mom has a whistle that can be heard on the moon!

Growing up on the farm, we woke up between 5:30 a.m. and 6:30 a.m. every morning to feed livestock and get ready for school. After school, we would go to the barn, get the horses saddled, cattle in the roping pen, goats on the lead, barrels set up and everything ready, and practice each one of our events for about four hours. We would then clean pens and feed the livestock until we heard the "whistle."

Please understand, I am not talking about a singsong whistle. No matter where you were on the farm, fairgrounds, grocery store, the next state, you could hear that "whistle," and you had better come running! It was such a distanced sound that the horses would hear it and come running from the back pasture! It was a call to dinner, a warning that the truck was started and the rig was pulling out of the rodeo grounds, a sound that meant help was needed. But most importantly, it was a sound that always brought you home.

Legacy is the sound that brings you home.

HONORING LEGACY

Everyone wants to believe they are part of something bigger than themselves. Knowing your family lineage is part of that. It's figuring out where you come from and understanding that you impact future generations!

Many limit their understanding of legacy to monetary inheritances, but that's only part of the picture. Money helps with bills, food, and putting gas in the

Honor Your Roots

gas tank. But to me, legacy also includes the memories, accomplishments, teachings, and beliefs handed down from generation to generation. It's how your family lineage traveled to be in the place where you were born. How they lived. How they worshipped. How they worked. And how they interacted with the world around them.

I also think legacy involves things like conflict resolution, work ethic, knowing what's important in life, giving and serving, but ultimately loving God with all my heart. That's important because it sets the stage for those I impact to let them know it's healthy to rely on God for redemption in times when we fail.

Maybe my great, great greats didn't know it at the time, but what they did created legacy that impacts me today. From revolting against religion and coming to America, forging mountain passes to new areas of discovery, and homesteading in Colorado during the Civil War, to fighting for our freedom in WWI and WWII. It's in my blood to fight for justice, work hard, and care for the ones I love. I have a fiery passion for justice from my mom, a steadfast way of being from my dad, and a deep caring for others that I know comes from my grandmother.

Because my parents were open and honest about their past and experiences, I was able to learn from their mistakes and successes. I'm thankful they were there for me when I made mistakes. I learned that when negative

GO

things happen, we shouldn't dwell on it. My parents taught me to deal with the mistake and find a way through God's wisdom and healing to move past it. There is always a solution—you just need to be willing to let God help you find it. Avoid using the word "can't" and figure out what you *can*!

Our legacy is a platform for future generations to grow from, create from, and live life from.

I'm a parent, so of course I write from the context and example of being a parent. But legacy applies to any relationship that has an authoritative impact in another's life. Teachers, mentors, pastors, coaches, and others leave legacies to those who follow.

Have you ever caught yourself saying, "Wow, I just sounded like my father/mother?" or "I just reacted exactly how my father/mother would have." It's because you have been impacted by them.

The conversations your children, grandchildren, family, and friends have is about what you did, how you acted, the fond memories, how you touched their hearts, and who you are as a person.

Look, don't think I've got it all together. I am far from perfect! I continually ask God to cover my failings.

I have the habit of getting very angry when things are not put away. I can be very harsh and the tone of my voice degrading. I mean, I will clean rather than spending time with my family. I'm not sure why I think I can demand perfection in a house with two kids under the age of six and two large, hairy dogs—but I do.

I have heard my five-year-old use the same tone I've used with her two-year-old sister, and I was grieved that I was responsible for this situation. I went to them and asked for forgiveness. We prayed and I let them know that I loved them very much no matter what our house looks like. You see, I am learning to let God work on me so I can let that perfection go and be a better example to my kiddos in actions and words.

What it comes down to is that I don't want the stories shared about me to be, "Remember how mom was always such a clean freak?" That's not the legacy I want to leave.

Legacy goes deep.

So many of us clean ourselves up on the outside, making our "house" look good but neglect the precious intimacy we could have with each other or God. Maybe if I had been playing with my kiddos, making the mess *with* them, and letting them help me clean up after, I would have taught them it's ok to have fun, make a mess, and clean it up so they could do it again later.

Here is another example of leaving the wrong kind of legacy. Have you ever said a bad word and the child repeated it a few seconds later? I have! How embarrassing is that?

GO

On the other side, I have also seen my toddler raise her hands when we listen to worship songs and sing at the top of her lungs. I've seen my kindergartener rush over to help a kid with a learning disorder when he needed it. I've seen my girls dance around our living room with contagious laughter, hug each other goodnight, encourage each other to try new things, and pray to Jesus that lost things would be found.

That is the legacy I pray to leave them.

When my life ends, I pray they will grow from my legacy—not be held back by it. Someday when they catch themselves acting like me, I hope it will be them showing God's love. Hopefully, they learn from watching me draw out the greatness God has instilled in others. I pray they grow from seeing their mom impact thousands of people singing and speaking about God's love. My greatest hope is that they'll think, "If my mom can do that, I can do it too, and so much more."

I want them to learn from watching me turn to Jesus and pray for help when I fail or lose my temper. And when dire situations arise, I hope they have steadfast confidence that God has everything under control and allow Him to comfort and perform the miraculous.

Choose to leave a legacy of powerful moments where others' experiences are of you as the superhero God created you to be. Let your legacy be built on the

Honor Your Roots

times you stepped in with God's wisdom to conquer difficult circumstances or kept going when all logic said it was impossible.

Take a good look at what you are doing now—the good, the bad, and the ugly. The circumstances, experiences, training, and how you deal with life, are all part of the legacy you will leave for others.

We can be examples to others in how to grow financially, emotionally, and spiritually, praying that God covers shortcomings in our lives. If we can instill in others what we've learned throughout life, maybe they won't have to learn things the hard way. Our hope is that generations to come can grow above and beyond what we have accomplished!

Set your legacy platform high, knowing that what you leave behind will impact those that come after you. The legacy to the next generation is your character woven through the stories and moments that made up your life.

Hold onto the moments that move you forward. Let go of the ones that hold you back. Embrace a legacy of the positive. The memory of "My favorite time of day" came after a hard day's work. The whistle called me home.

I remember what my parents did for me and the sacrifices they made so that I could be successful. They taught me that God is always in the story. He will always provide and always cover my failings. There's a sense of pride in how I grew up and knowing who I am. It drives me to continue my family's legacy. Knowing what my ancestors fought for, and the good or bad that came with it, shows me who I am.

So, when you look back, don't forget to remember the sacrifice of past generations. Be mindful of what you've been given and find comfort in it. This is legacy.

HONORING YOUR FAMILY LEGACY

Decide how you will honor your family's legacy. The name you carry has greatness in it. Offer grace to those in your past. There is always good and bad. By understanding the failings and successes of those in your family line, you can give yourself grace and embrace hope in your future.

Decide what to do with what you learn from your family history. You choose what your story will be, and you can choose what to leave your family. Remember God covers mistakes with his overwhelming love and grace.

Here are a few ways you can choose to leave your legacy in everyday life:

- Read scriptures every day. They tell you who you are and help you move forward in your life.

Honor Your Roots

- Pray every day! Bring God into every situation and ask for His guidance.
- Be intentional in every action with the understanding that you are impacting those around you.
- Be grateful every morning. Get up and decide what you are grateful for. There is *always* something to be thankful for.
- Write affirmations to yourself every day. It doesn't have to reflect what's really going on in your life, but doing it reminds you who God says you are and what you are worth.
- Choose to focus on the positive—it sets the tone for your mindset throughout your day.
- Respect your family name and those who came before you. Honor where they came from and what they did in their life. If you know your legacy and who you are, you will have a better understanding of yourself.

These things may not change your circumstances, but they can have a powerful impact on your mindset and how you choose to walk through those circumstances. These actions compound over time and create moments in others' lives that instill God's greatness in them. Just think—One day you can be someone's "whistle" bringing them home!

GO

Questions to Go:

1. Our legacy is a platform for future generations to grow from, create from, and live life from. What are two or three traits that make up the platform previous generations gave you?
2. What are some of the circumstances, experiences, training, and life skills that are part of the legacy you will leave for others?
3. Think about those around you. Who are you influencing? Who will benefit from your legacy?

CHAPTER 7

What is a Home

A SECRET PLACE

To me, a home is different than a house. Usually you search for a house to make a home. So, what is the difference between a house and a home?

Houses come in many forms. They are usually made up of at least four walls and a roof and come in different sizes, shapes, and amenities. A typical house could be built of wood or brick. It could be a mobile home, or an apartment building. On the road in the rodeo world, it would consist of the living quarters on the horse trailer or a tent by the stalls. Still, there was always a place to go back to that had the permanent title of home.

Homes are different than houses. More than a structure, they are made up of the people within the walls and under the roof. You can have a house, but you cannot have a home without the people who live there.

GO

In our home, Christmas was a celebration of Jesus' birth. I LOVE Christmas lights! LOVE, LOVE, LOVE! I loved the way they looked, how they made me feel, and the season they represented—how they lit up the dark! Later in life, I would realize the relation of the lights to the light from a bright star lighting the way for the wise men to Jesus. When I was little, I would beg my dad to put up lights for Christmas, but he never did. He didn't say anything at the time, but it was because we couldn't afford them. So he would take us into town to see the lights on other homes, city streets, and the Old Town Square of Fort Collins.

It was my freshman year of college, and I headed back home for the holidays. As my sister and I turned the corner down the country road to our house, I started to cry. There was a single strand of Christmas lights wrapped around a fence post welcoming us home. And that is an example of the difference between a house and a home—the people we love and the memories we cherish.

In real estate, that same concept translates into the desires and the wants of the people we work with. Homes usually include all five senses combined into one space, and include pain or pleasure. I believe the experience in a home should be as beautiful as Christmas lights are to me. It should be a safe place where the individuals in that

What is a Home

space are free to be comforted, rest, hide, and be loved for who they are.

Physical and emotional storms happen in everyone's lives. Home should be a place to run to for comfort and shelter. Homes should offer security when things get difficult. Homes are where we celebrate, and they offer us peace and rest.

Homes should be places of sanctuary and love, where honesty is welcomed. They are where you are free to create vision, passion, and dream big dreams.

Every home should be a place of physical or emotional intimacy. And when I say "intimacy," I'm not just referring to the intimacy between husband and wife. It's related to all relationships. Relationships bring intimacy through the stories and experiences of the people that live in the home and through the people who come into the home.

When these things are removed, a hollowness enters, the lights turn off, and the home simply becomes a house.

HOW TO MAKE YOUR HOME A REFUGE

Our real estate team is founded on values that drive every decision we make and the way we interact with our clients. It is summed up in our vision statement which

GO

is: "We are a community of exceptional real estate agents, living an elite lifestyle of dreaming big, playing big and providing a better future for our raving fans."

My top values drive how I interact with others. They are faith and family, authenticity and integrity, forgiveness, joy, understanding, communication, and commitment. When working with a client to find a home, I find out what their values are. That way, I can help them find a house they can bring those values into and make it their home.

Let me share an experience that instilled in me integrity, understanding, and forgiveness. It's one example of how my home was a place of refuge.

I was a junior in high school, at the top of all rodeo events I was competing in, and the Broncos were going to the Superbowl! YEAH! I was invited to a friend's house to watch the Superbowl. My car was in the shop, so my dad let me borrow his with one instruction: DO NOT, under any circumstance, go downtown after the game! "Ok daddy!" I said as I headed to my friend's house.

The Broncos won and the town was electrified. We got wrapped up in the moment and my brain seemed to have a major lapse in judgment. I found myself downtown in his car surrounded by a crowd. I was terrified. As I drove through the crowd, they began rocking the car back and forth. I panicked and pushed on, probably a bit

What is a Home

faster than I should have and WHAM! A body fell into the front window and smashed the glass. Oh, the horror and dread! The person was okay, but I thought my father was going to kill me.

At home, I inspected the damage. Dented fenders and a shattered front window are kinda hard to hide, so I came up with the perfect story. That night for the first time, I lied through my teeth about what had happened. My father knew I was lying but had no proof, so off to bed I went. As I lay in bed, anxiety came over me. I ran out of my room crying, fell on the couch beside him, spilled the truth, and waited.

His response? A hug. Wait … what? He hugged me, said he was thankful I came home safe, and sent me to bed with the understanding that he and my mom would let me know the consequences later.

I disobeyed in a huge way and caused major damage to my dad's car, but he responded with love. There were no outbursts of anger or raised voices. Yes, there would be a punishment, but it came in the form of a life lesson, not an anger outburst. Our home was a safe place to tell the truth.

Needless to say, I didn't dare ask to go out with friends or stay late at school. I stuck to my chores and waited … and waited … and waited. When the rodeo season started again, he came to me and let me know that

GO

because of my disobedience, I would not be attending the first three rodeos of the season. What?! That could put my National Championship qualification at a huge risk! But this punishment shaped me.

Our home was a place of integrity, honor, and authenticity.

Most of all, our home was a place of refuge where it was okay to make mistakes, grow, learn, and know that we are always loved.

Maybe your home is not a place where you are living the life you value. If that's the case, here are some things you can do to change that.

Start by choosing to make it different!

We need to ask for wisdom in every situation. When faced with my disobedience, my father prayed for God's wisdom and direction in the discipline, so that I would learn a lesson through love and not judgment. But to hear God, we need alone time with Him. Scripture calls us to have a "secret place" to pray. We are called into deep relationship with our Creator and need to have this space where we can retreat and be with Him.

This isn't just a command, but it is a lifegiving practice! Is there a place you go to think, relax, or create? Maybe you take a run to settle your mind or love to hike because you see the beauty in nature. When I was younger, I would go out to the pasture, climb on my horse, lie back, and look up at the stars. Now, my place is a chair in my living room by the fireplace. Oh, how times change.

There's intimacy in prayer and spending time in the Word of God. I strongly encourage you to find your secret place with God in your home. Whether it's a specific room or a quiet corner, have a place where you can read or just be with Him. Make this space a "secret place" where you can receive healing and comfort as you spend time there.

My secret place is an important part of my life. There are many times God uses this place when I am angry, not sleeping well, not feeling well, feeling overwhelmed, or discouraged to remind me of His love. When I need a vision for my family and business, or when I am not living in the abundance He has called me to, I go to my secret place.

In that chair, I sit and pray, and it brings me back to the quiet, peaceful moments I need. These are times that remind me how blessed I am to have a roof over my head, a fireplace to keep me warm, and space to be myself. It is in these moments I recognize that I am loved unconditionally. I am reminded of the vision He placed in my heart, and I usually come away with clarity and a next-steps action plan!

When you are in your quiet place, ask God for a clear vision of what your home should be.

GO

Some homes have specific purposes and, therefore, specific requirements. Some homes offer shelter to those in need. Some homes are gathering places. Some homes are places to learn. And some homes are simply places where family can be together. There is beauty in all of it. Ask God to clarify your needs versus your wants.

Write down the vision for your home. Make a vision board—and don't forget to dream big! Ask yourself what your perfect home would be. What are the things of value you need in your home? The values behind the vision will drive the "why" and the why will help you focus on what's really needed in your home.

Once you have the overall vision, go deeper. Ask God to give you dreams of how the different spaces in your home could be used. Look, I get that our prayers are not about getting everything we want, but why not ask? God promises to give us the desires of our hearts. When you spend time with Him, He places those desires in you. Remember, the life desires He placed in your heart are far above and beyond anything you could dream up on your own.

It's also a good idea to meet with your family and invite them into the process. Establish communication so everyone can participate. What is their vision? Start determining what your family spaces should look like.

What is a Home

We work from home a lot and our oldest child approached us one day letting us know that it seemed we ignore her and "work too much." I don't ever want my children to feel neglected! I went to my space and prayed. I came away with clarity in one of my values, family.

I sat down with her, and we chatted a bit. I let her know how valuable she is to me and why we worked so much. Going to Disney World is a dream she has been holding onto for a while. I let her know that we wanted to give her that dream of going to Disney World. I then invited her into the process, and she began helping me print materials, track things on the white board and "work" with me. By helping her become part of the process, she began to understand why she had to play quietly when I was on the phone. But most importantly, I realized the importance of sticking to a work schedule that allowed me grace to stop and spend time with her.

Be honest with your family about expectations, wants, and needs. Laugh, cry, celebrate, and do life together!

This kind of thoughtful approach to home buying or selling is why we are passionate about real estate. Real estate starts with land. A house improves the land, but the home should be an improvement to your life.

Think about it. Everything starts within your home. It's where you wake up and start your day to go out and

GO

meet the world. If all else fails, you can always come back home. That's where you find a place of peace. One day we'll be home with Christ. Here on earth, our home should be the closest we get to that.

Big or small, home is about providing a better future for the people living there. Home should come from a heartbeat, not a dollar bill. Money doesn't create the memories. Memories are made through the smell of a home-cooked meal, the sound of a child playing, and the loving experiences. Home is the laughter and love shared between the walls in a house.

Know this—making the home a refuge begins with you.

Speak out something positive every day. There is power in your words!

Proverbs 18:21 "Death and life are in the power of the tongue, and those who love it will eat its fruit."

For example, say things like: "I am grateful that I slept well!" "I am grateful for hot water!" "I am grateful for my work." Doing this sets the tone for your day, and you are teaching your brain to be positive.

Dream big about your home, and let God do the rest. Above all else, start your day spending time in your secret place.

What is a Home

Questions to Go:

1. The people we love, and the memories we cherish are what make the difference between a house and a home. What are the memories and people that make up your home?
2. The values that drive how I interact with others are faith and family, authenticity and integrity, forgiveness, joy, understanding, communication, and commitment. What are two or three of your top values?
3. Scripture calls us to have a "secret place" to pray and be alone with God. Why do you think we need to be alone to hear Him?

Conclusion

My cancer journey could have become the thing that kept me stuck. It could have made me bitter, fearful, or made me question God. I'm thankful it did not. Instead, the thing that was meant for evil (Genesis 50:20), God used to strengthen and bless me—and my family.

In reality, I have experienced some side effects from the chemo.

The steroids killed my hip joints. I've struggled through the pain and recovery of six hip surgeries. But the good news is I am up and walking! You might even say I'm bionic!

I was told I would never have children and yet today have two beautiful, healthy girls. Our oldest daughter is our miracle child because despite the negative diagnosis, her birth proves God is faithful.

Our second is our redemption child because I was diagnosed with cancer on November 17, 1998 at the age of seventeen. On November 17, 2016 I had a tumor removed off my brain because of the radiation I had when I was seventeen. And God redeemed that date with our second daughter who was born on November 17, 2017.

I love words that inspire, and one of my favorite quotes is this one:

> *"There is no doubt that it is around the family and the home that all the greatest virtues, the most dominating virtues of human, are created, strengthened and maintained." – Winston Churchill*

I like it because it sums up everything I believe about family and home. Home is a sacred place where we grow, learn, laugh, and live together. Home is where we learn to be who we are meant to be.

We are all unique, but our true gifts and purpose are only uncovered when we willingly work and walk with God. By showing compassion toward others, allowing Dunamis in our lives to impact the world around us, we live as the true superheroes God has made us all to be.

Honor your roots and leave a legacy of hope for future generations to build on. Let your story be one of God's love, and in that way, carry on your family's legacy, and establish your home.

Most of all, know God will walk with you through life's challenges and celebrations. He is the source to live life to the fullest in all you do. There will always be

Conclusion

storms. But remember that when we invite God into the storm, the end of the story is—we win!

Finally ...

"If you are going to live, leave a legacy. Make a mark on the world that can't be erased." – Author Unknown

About the Author

BRANDI ASPINALL

"Building Relationships for a Better Future."

A fifth generation Colorado native, Brandi is happily married and has two beautiful girls. She has a bachelor degree in Technical Journalism/Public Relations from Colorado State University and is a founding member of Living Colorado Elite, one of Berkshire Hathaway HomeServices award winning teams. She has sung at Disneyland, national championship rodeos, church services and the Caesar's Palace Colosseum in Las Vegas. She has spoken at the National High School Finals Rodeo, multiple church events and services since she was seventeen. Through ministry and speaking she brings an experiential knowledge to the table and is able to relate in an authentic way with the people she interacts with. Whether through singing, coaching or sports, her focus is serving others and encouraging them to play

GO

big in life. From world champion in the rodeo arena to cancer survivor to top realtor within her company, she has a passion for uplifting and motivating others to ignite the greatness within themselves and living a full life in Christ.

Email: brandi@livingcoelite.com
Website: www.livingcoelite.com